KINDLE PAPERWHITE USER GUIDE

The 2021 Complete User Manual On How To Master Kindle Paperwhite 10th Generation E-Reader Tablet For Beginners And Seniors With Reading Tips And Tricks

Thomas Mallack

Copyright © 2021 All rights Reserve

No part of this book shall be reproduced, stored in a retrieval system, or transmitted by any means, electronic, mechanical, photocopying, recording, or otherwise, without written permission from the publisher. Although every precaution has been taken in the preparation of this book, the publisher and author assume no responsibility for errors or omissions. Nor is any liability assumed for damages resulting from the use of the information contained herein.

LEGAL NOTICE:

This book is copyright protected and is only for personal use. This book should not be amended or distributed, sold, quote, or paraphrased without the consent of the author or publisher.

DISCLAIMER:

The information contained in this book is for educational purposes only. All efforts have been executed to present accurate, reliable, and up to date information. No warranties of any kind are implied. The contents from this book are derived from various sources. Please consult a licensed professional before attempting any techniques contained herein.

By reading this document, the reader agrees that under no circumstances is the author responsible for any losses, direct or indirect, which are incurred as a result of the information contained in this book including errors, omissions, and inaccuracy

Table of Contents

Introduction 1

Design and Visualization 2

Operating your Kindle 6

    Turn on your Kindle 9

    Reading a Book 10

    Creating a collection 15

Update Kindle 17

Sleep Mode 22

Font size and style 24

Change Password 29

Methods to delete books 34

How to print 42

PDF in Kindle 47

How to connect a TV 56

Setup Bluetooth connectivity 59

Bluetooth Troubleshoot 62

Wi-Fi Connection 64

Borrowing library's books 66

Send books from Mac ... 68

Move iPad Books to Kindle ... 71

Synchronizing Kindle to iPad ... 74

Create Kindle Child profile ... 75

Edit Child Profile ... 76

Bookmark and Highlight Content ... 76

Word Wise ... 80

Kindle PaperWhite reset ... 81

Troubleshooting ... 83

Freezing Issues ... 89

Introduction

Since 2015 I abandoned my Kindle, I didn't remember much about them; the one I used, had a full keyboard in the lower part which was hard to navigate and no backlight, and it was impossible to read in the dark. In my mind, Kindles were old relics. But this summer, when I saw one of my most trendy friends using his Paperwhite, I was convinced that I could enter the Kindle realm. It was still a Kindle, but in his hands, it looked so cool, much smaller and sleeker than I remembered with just one button down to turn it on. He enjoyed it, he guaranteed me, especially on a journey, and by then I became overwhelmed by the mounds of books that were littered on my floor. Really, I thought I could take a shot of the Paperwhite on PrimeDay, and I am so happy to do so.

Many of the problems I encountered with the older Kindle generation were completely removed with Paperwhite. It is incredibly light, yet it's not a button rather a responsive touch screen. I can hold it and flip with one hand on the next page; I can read even when I hold my pole and smush between my fellow transit passengers. I can also enter my already filled work rucksack much easier than a 300-page book, which means I read more because I have my book with me all the time.

Moreover, it is a delight to use in fact. "I don't feel like I am looking at a computer screen, with the backlight and the matt finish." The Kindle screen has no glare - unlike my phone display or even laptop - which is amazingly peaceful when I read in my bed before I fall asleep. And the backlight means that even if all the lights are off, I can read it. The latest is even waterproof and is protected in two meters of water for up to 60 minutes.

Design and Visualization

The Kindle Paperwhite has been designed as the mid-range e-reader for Amazon, sits in the Amazon range between the inexpensive Kindle and the super-class Kindle Oasis. It does not feel like the Oasis, especially since it has a plastic back, but we could easily hold it and it doesn't look horrible. All that said, with fingerprints on the back, we quickly noticed it was a bit rough.

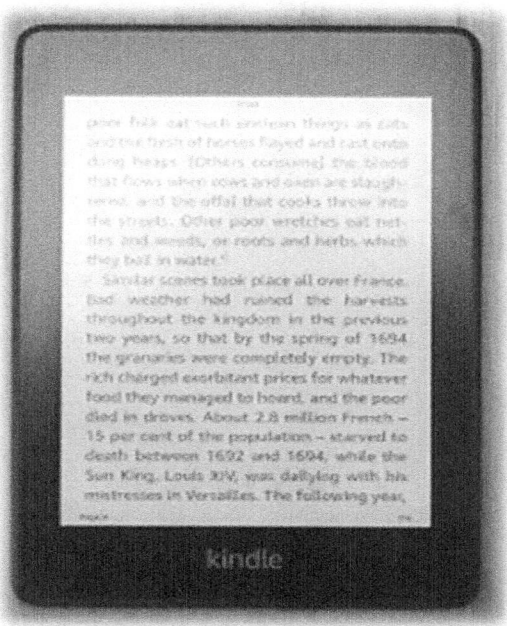

The power button and the micro-USB port on the bottom side are available to charge, and the sides are devoid of buttons hence, you can handle the gadget comfortably without making a pressing mistake. The device is can easily be handled.

The Bezels around the display are, however, thicker than on some expensive e-readers. They are set flush with the display and give the Paperwhite a high-end aesthetic and making it look comparable to the Kindle Voyage. One thing left out is that no physical buttons are available to change the page. Rather, you will flip the pages with the touchscreen. This is very reactive to the touch, so you won't fight to move through your pages.

It has a display of 6 inches with a 300-pixel resolution per inch, just as the previous Paperwhite, which is the optimum text read resolution. The luminosity has improved here slightly, although we did not detect this. That said, the latest Kindle Paperwhite is already bright enough, but you could only appreciate it if you read on a beach lounger.

You may wrap the Kindle Paperwhite in one of five cases if you wish to change its appearance. There are fabric alternatives and even two leather options, and the complete variety may be seen here.

The material is twinned from £24.99 / $29.99 /AU$44.95 with a leather base of £34.99 / $39.99 / AU$54.95. These are available at Amazon. The Kindle Paperwhite in black or Twilight Blue is also available for you. The Kindle Paperwhite now works with a water-resistant body built which is one of the few features from the super tech Oasis. This means that, without worries, you may easily read in the bathroom or while sitting by the pool. It can tolerate 2 meters depth of water for up to 60 minutes.

Operating your Kindle

Know the hardware features of the Kindle. You need to be aware of just two major hardware elements, both near the bottom of the housing of the Kinder:

Power button – Used to switch the Kindle on and off this small, round button. The "Kindle" logo is on the right.

Charging port – This little rectangular port is used for battery charging. On the left side of the "Kindle" logo, you will locate it.

Comprehensive interaction with elements on the screen. You can choose options on the screen of your Kindle by tapping them like any other tablet. By taping a text field (e.g. search bar), a keyboard that may be used to write information will be created on the screen.

If necessary, Charge your Kindle. If the Kindle is not yet powered, plug one end of a cable into one electrical outlet (or, if the wall adapter is lacking, a charging USB port into a computer), then plug it into the micro-USB port at the bottom of the Kindle. The duration of your Kindle battery will be determined by things like screen brightness, usage frequency, and app running.

Turn on your Kindle

Switch on your Kindle. To do that, hold the Power button at the lower part of the Kindle. This will trigger it to switch on when your Kindle is off or sleeping. The power button should be pressed for around 7 seconds until the Kindle's screen appears blank if you have to switch your kindle off. Kindle is prompted to restart with the power button holding down for 20 seconds.

If necessary, go to the Home Screen. You can reach the home screen by touching on the top of the screen, then tap the Home symbol in the house-like form if your kindle opens to something other than the Home screen.

Click on Kindle Set Up. This is on the home display. The setup menu is created for this.

Follow the on-screen instructions. While the order of information that you need to enter may change, for each of the following features you typically need to fill the forms:

Language — Select your preferred language.

Date and time — Choose the time zone, the area, the date, and/or the time locally.

Wi-Fi – After choosing a Wi-Fi network, enter the password as required.

Amazon Account — Input the email address and passcode of your Amazon account to sign in using your Kindle.

Reading a Book

If necessary, go back to Home Screen. Just tap on the top of the screen, and tap the Home icon in the house.

Tap My items. Click My items which can be found at the top of the display. You will see a menu. Skip this and the next step if you want anything else besides a book (e.g., a magazine).

Tap Books. The menu is here. This makes the contents of your home screen show books alone.

Choose a book. Tap the book that you'd want to read. This takes you to the last page that you had opened.

Turn one page. To move to the next page, tap the center of the screen.

Return a page. Click on the far-left side of the screen if you want to move to the page above.

View toolbar. Tap the toolbar at the top of the Kindle screen. From the top of the screen, you will notice this toolbar drop.

Check the content of the toolbar. While the contents of the toolbar can differ based on what you read, the following options normally appear between left and right:

Home – You are going back to your home screen when you tap this house-shaped icon.

Back — The reverse arrow-shaped icon returns a page (for instance, if you're in a menu, press it returns to the final page of the menu).

Brightness – By tapping this bulb-shaped symbol, you can drag a slider left and right to reduce or enhance the brightness of your Kindle.

Store – The eBook Store will be opened to purchase new content by tapping the cart-like icon.

Search — The search bar which is like a glass magnifier icon, is used to search a book (or open page) for a certain word or sentence.

Menu — Taping this 3-line icon will reveal the menu from where many Kindle choices can be selected (e.g., Settings).

Secondary menu options that display when reading a book are Aa choice, the X-ray option, the Go-To option, and the Share option. Go To and X-Ray allows you to search your book for particular options and share links with social media while Aa open font preferences.

If necessary, go back to Home Screen. Tap the top of the panel to open the toolbar and then tap on the house-shaped home symbol after you are ready to return to the Home Screen of your book.

Creating a collection

1. what is a collection. In essence, a collection is a folder where a bunch of books is stored. The development of a collection might help to clear your Kindle home screen if you have a group of books you would like to arrange.

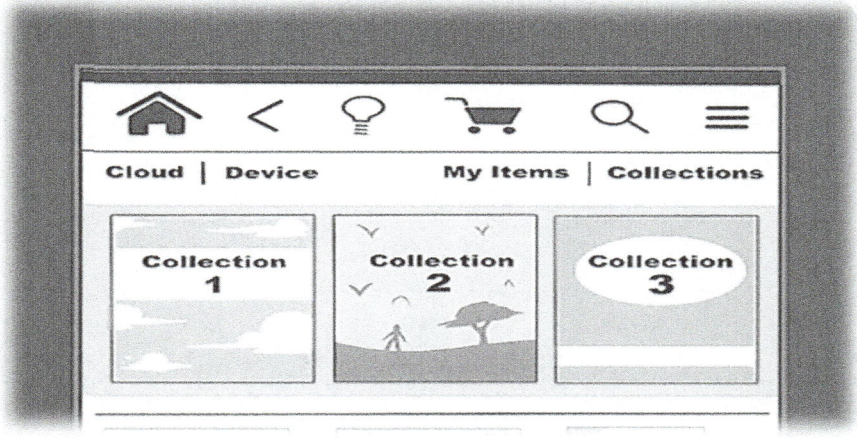

2 Go to the Screen of Home. To open the Home Screen, tap the top of the screen and tap the Home symbol in the house form.

Tap the 3 horizontal lines. It's at Home Screen's upper right-hand corner. There's a menu. You may have to click the upper part of the screen to open the toolbar.

Tap New Collection creation. This is on the menu. This opens up a list of your books.

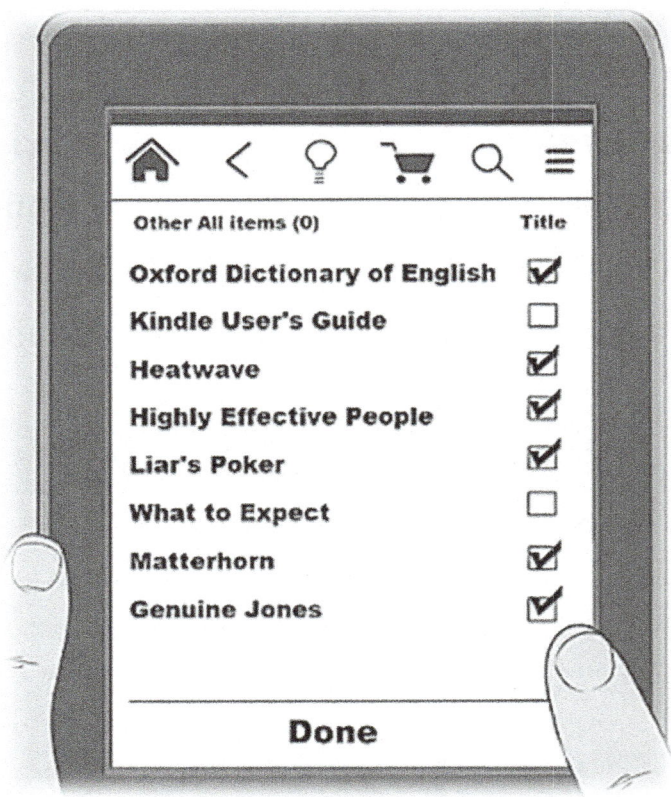

5. **Choose books to add.** Click on the name of each book in your collection you want to include. After each book you tap, you should see a checkmark.

6. **Touch Done.** It's at the upper part of the display. This saves you and adds books to your collection. By tapping it on, you may view the collection on the home screen.

Update Kindle

Kindle's Software is routinely updated by Amazon with bug patches, upgrades, and also new features like book-cover displays. Here is how to constantly be up-to-date with yours.

See your kindle software

When charging and creating a Wi-Fi connection, your Kindle should download automatically and update itself. Your Kindle may not be operating the latest software, however, you can set your Kindle is in Airplane mode, not to have it linked to the internet later on.

Go to your home page of Kindle and tap the three small points on your right top to open the menu to see which version of your Kindle software currently works.

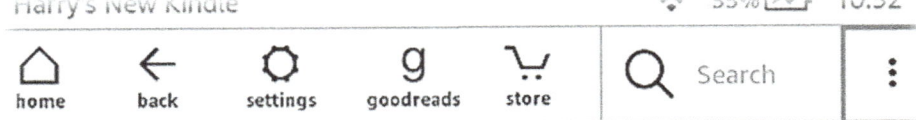

- In the menu of your Kindle, click on "Settings."
- On the Settings screen click "Device Options."
- To view information on the hardware and firmware your Kindle is using, tap "Device information."
- You can view the version your Kindle is running under "Firmware Version." You'll see that mine is on Kindle 5.13.5 in the screen photo below.

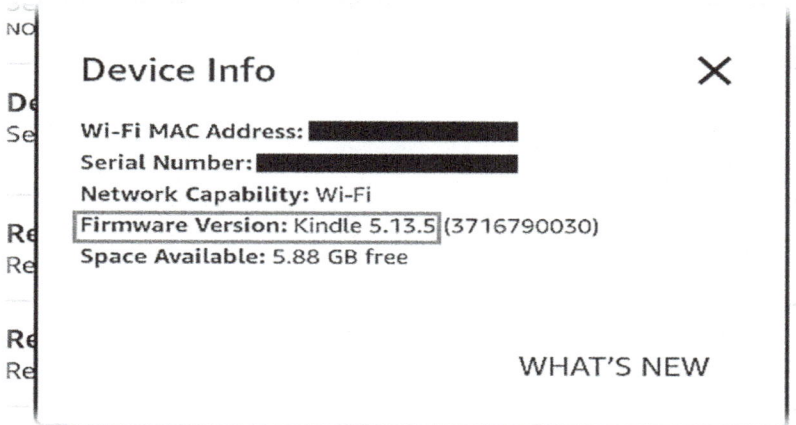

- When you know what your Kindle software includes, you have to compare it with the official release list. Check the Kindle software updates page for Amazon. See the version of your Kindle and compare your number with the current.

- I have a 10th generation Kindle Paper White, so my Kindle is up to date.

Wi-Fi update

If the latest software is not installed in your Kindle, you can upgrade it. To connect to Wi-Fi, first, connect your Kindle and charge it.

Tap the three small points on your Kindle 'Settings' screen.

Update manually

Download Update

With your Kindle's version number, PaperWhite 2 verified in our instance, navigate to the Amazon Fire & Kindle Software Updates page. Scroll down to the section Kindle and match your Kindle with the corresponding model. Recall, other variations of the same model may be available – that is why in step one we looked up the serial number. A download link will appear with the latest version number after the model is choosing. Note down the version number but don't download it yet.

Do a Confirmation of the version number of your Kindle and check if it is higher than the present version before you download the update. Navigate to Menu, then settings>

③ Menu > Device Information on your Kindle. Like the next one, you'll see a screen.

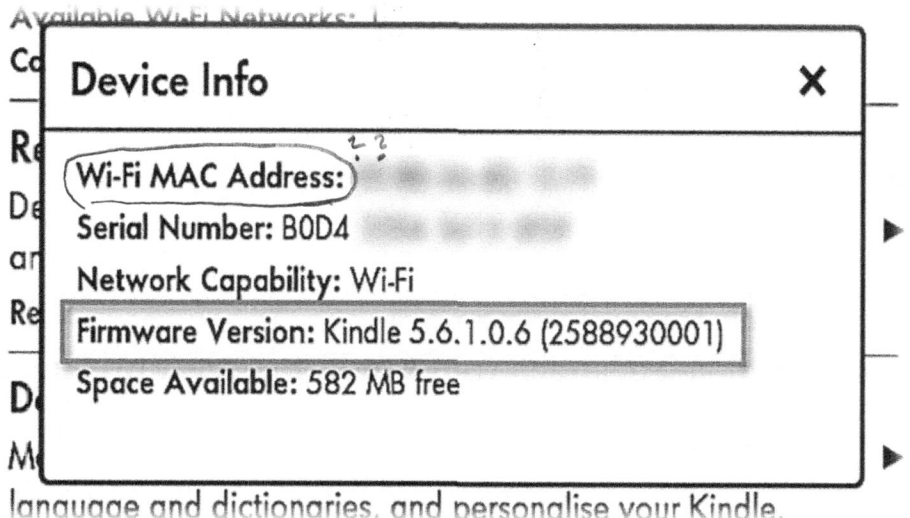

Clearly, on our Paperwhite the firmware type we have (5.6.1) is behind the most recently released version (5.8.5). We got the update from summer 2016 somewhere on this line but missed the huge upgrade in fall 2016 which introduced the new home screen layout. Now that we can obtain the update file with the disparity confirmed between the latest version and our version. Click on the "Software Update Download" link. The update is going to be saved as a .bin file.

Name	Date modified	Type	Size
.active_content_sandbox	11/25/2014 9:42 PM	File folder	
cache	1/17/2016 1:05 AM	File folder	
documents	11/16/2016 3:16 PM	File folder	
driveinfo.calibre	11/16/2016 10:22 ...	CALIBRE File	1 KB
metadata.calibre	11/16/2016 10:23 ...	CALIBRE File	11,619 KB
update_kindle_paperwhite_v2_5.8.5.0.2.bin	11/16/2016 10:17 ...	BIN File	204,787 KB

Copy and installation

Once downloaded, attach your Kindle Paperwhite using the USB cable to your computer and copy the .BIN update file to your Kindle Paperwhite's root directory. If the file is in the top folder, the copied update package path is F:\update kindle [version number].bin in case your PC mounts the Kindle as F drive

Sleep Mode

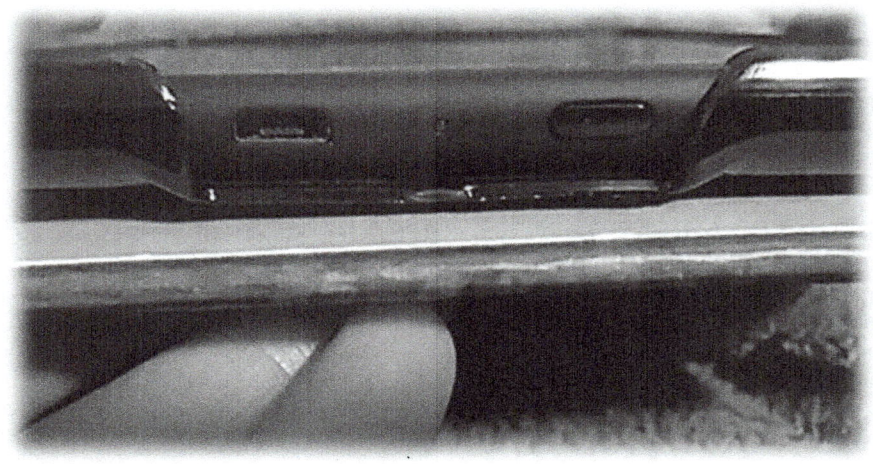

1. Please find the power button. On a Kindle Paperwhite, at the bottom of the device, on the right-hand side of the USB connector is the power button.

2. Switch off your paperwhite kindle. Click the power button as you want on a phone. A few times the green light flashes close to the power button and the screen becomes obscured and "paper" appears Your screen then becomes a book announcement or a telescope picture for a woman. Don't worry, your Kindle Paperwhite may seem like it, so your battery won't be utilized. So don't worry. You can disable

this advertising by heading to your Kindle's "Settings" section.

3) If you have one, close your case. This prevents your Kindle from crashing accidentally.

Font size and style

1 Decide what book you want to alter the font style. Tap on that book once you have chosen.

2 Tap your screen top. There should be a whole range of possibilities. To modify your font style, select "Aa."

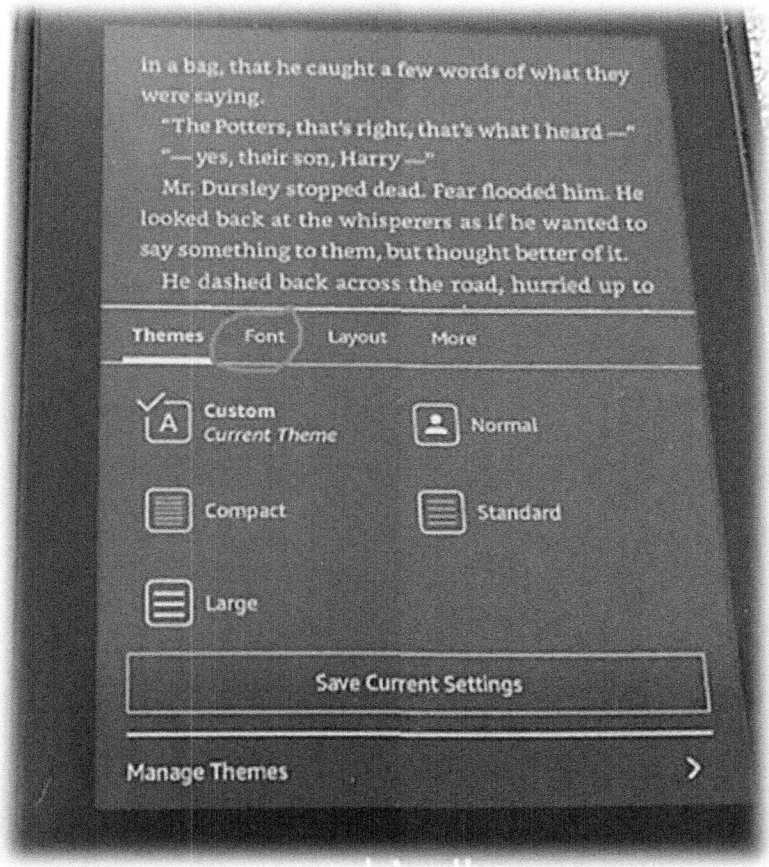

3 Choose "font." When you tap on "Aa," more suggestions will be available. The option "Font" will be selected.

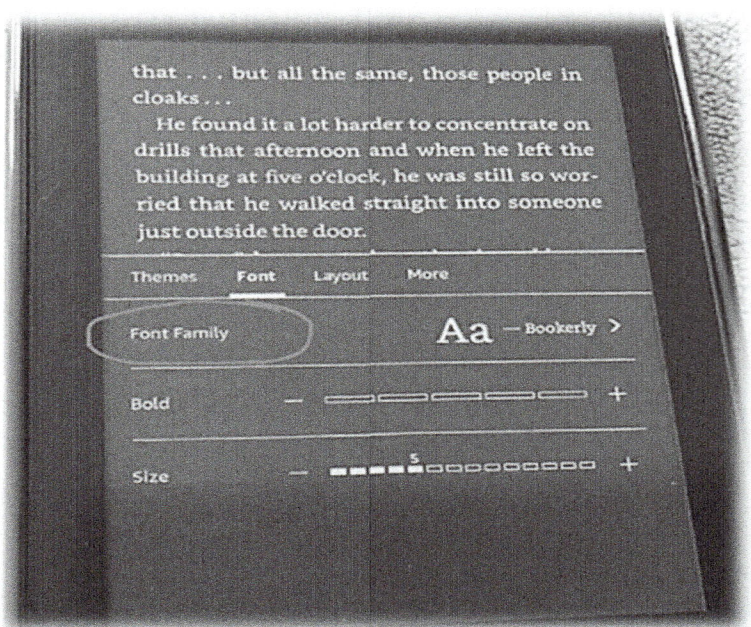

4 Tap on "Font family.". Once you choose "Font," when the following screen appears, you will want to pick "Font Family."

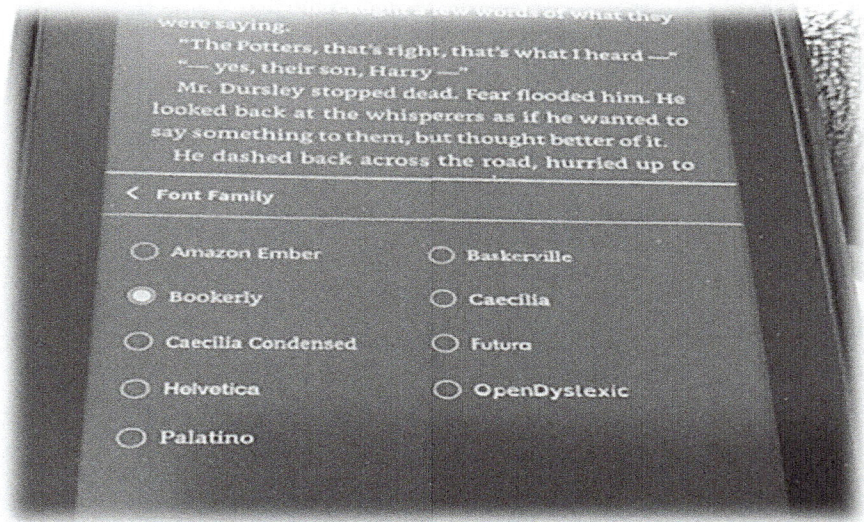

5 Select another font style. You should see multiple font styles when you click "Font Family." Select the one you like and then, tap "Font Family", with the back button on your screen, go back to your font options.

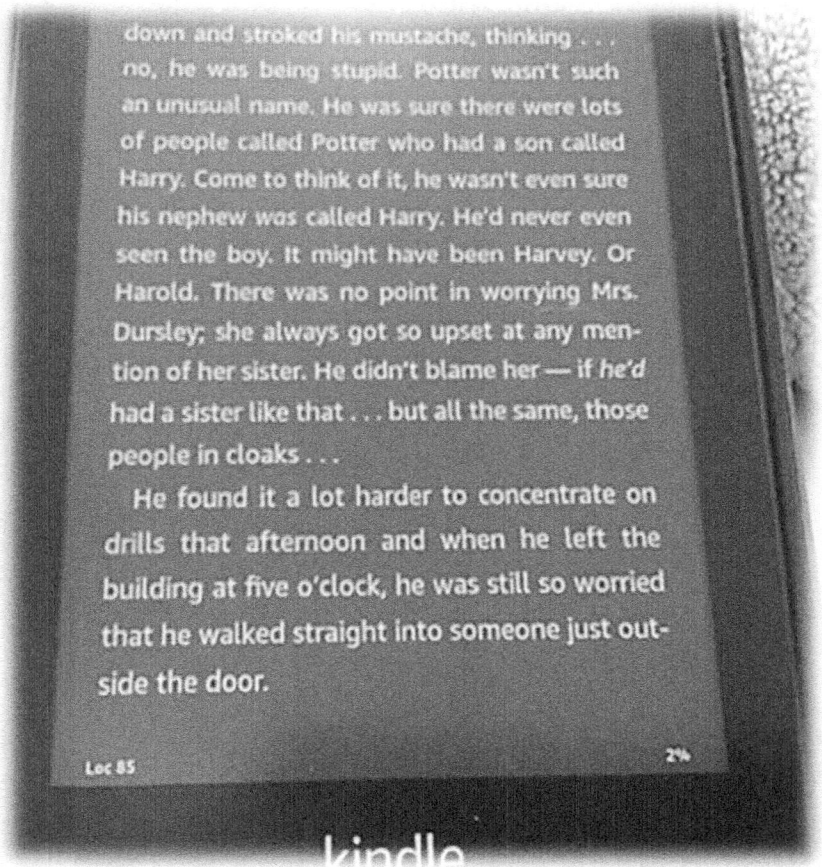

6 Move from options. To leave the options, click above the box and return to your book, which should now have a different font.

Font Size Modification

- Select the book with font size that you would prefer to change. Tap on that book.
- Click the screen's top. You will want to choose "Aa" in same way you would like to change the font style
- Choose "Font."

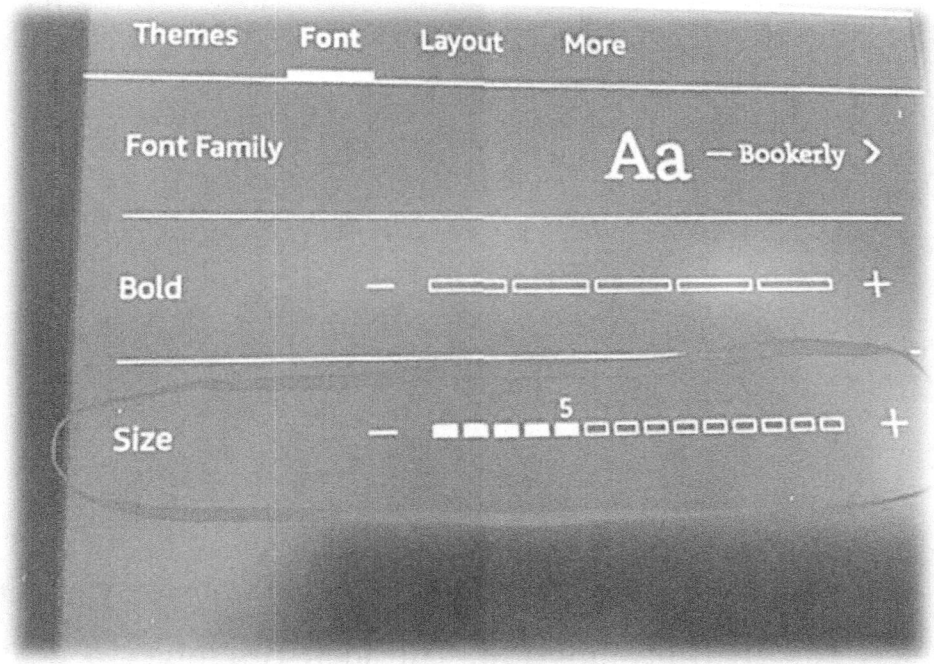

- Change the font size. The font size can be changed at the end of the "Font" page. To enlarge the font, or make it smaller, use the "+" button.
- Moe from options. Tap above the box and return to the book once the font size is modified to your preferences.

Change Password

Method 1-Password modification

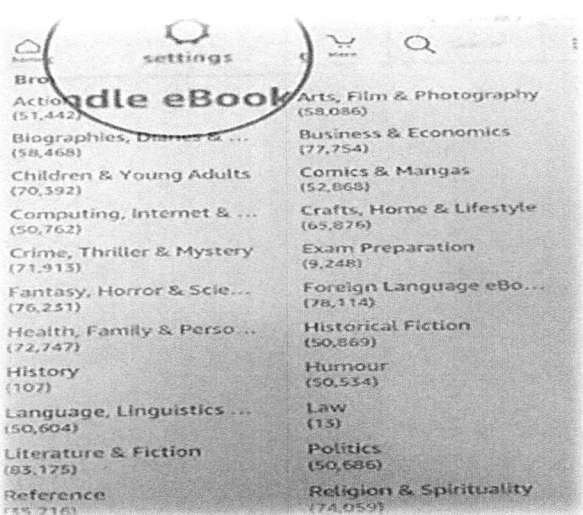

1 Go to Configuration. On the top of your website, you can select the "Settings" button. The icon resembles a gear. After hitting the "Settings" button, you will notice an icon that says "All Settings" at the top right of your website. Click that option.

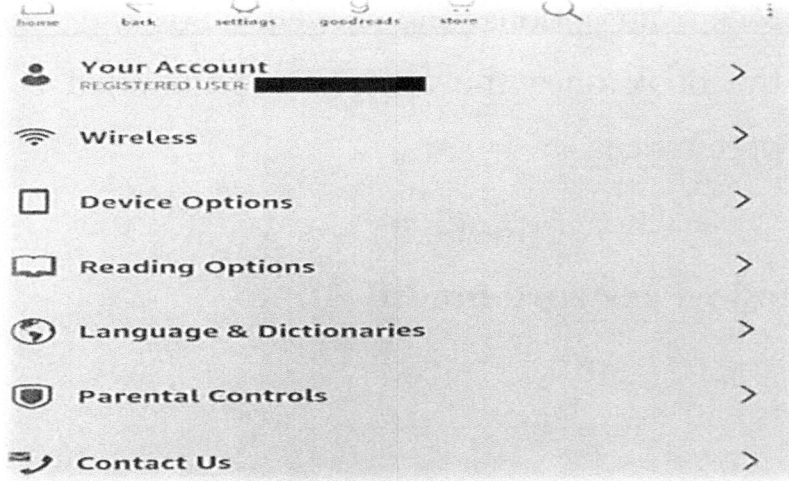

2 Click on the "Device Options" button. A new page with many options will be displayed. Tap on "Device Options."

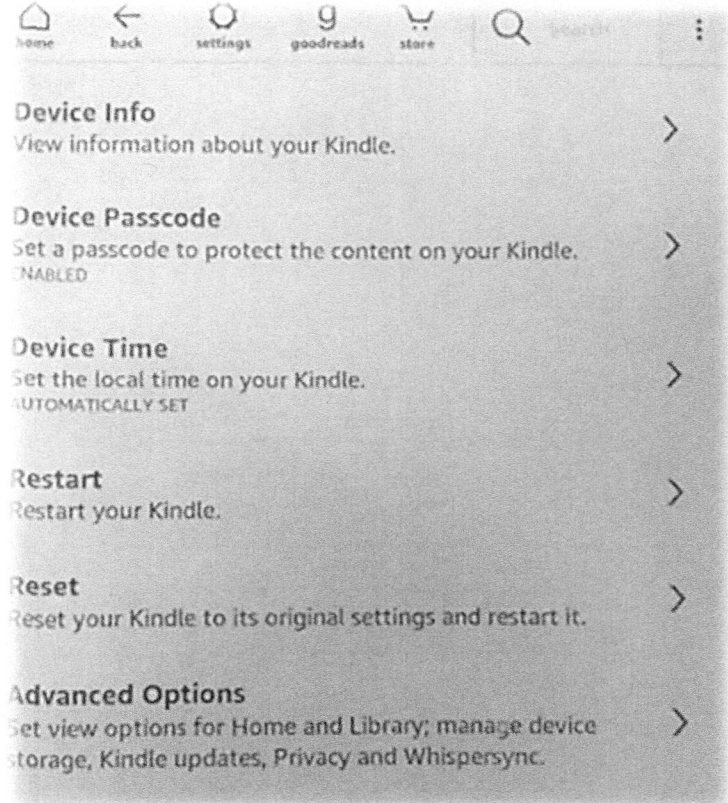

3 Select " Device Passcode." After you click the "Device Options" panel, a few further panels are found. A sub-page will be opened by clicking on "Device Passcode." Then a password can be created. Click "Change Passcode" if you have a password, and you would want to change it already. Enter and enable your current password. Confirm again.

Tip: Consider using the password for other accounts/devices that you have used. In this way, if you need it, it will be a lot easier to recall.

4 Switch the gadget off and see whether it works. Keep the passcode in mind if you do not usually use your kindle. You can put it down on a piece of paper.

Method 2 Change forgot Password

1 Try to remember. Given that a Kindle is not too dangerous to hack, you could have enabled a simple

password. Try to remember and enter. A good attempt is worth it!

2 Tap on "Forgotten Password" if your effort didn't work. You will open a sub-page to seek assistance here.

3 Keep adding details following the directions. Describe in more detail what you need.

Methods to delete books

Remove items from Content Library.

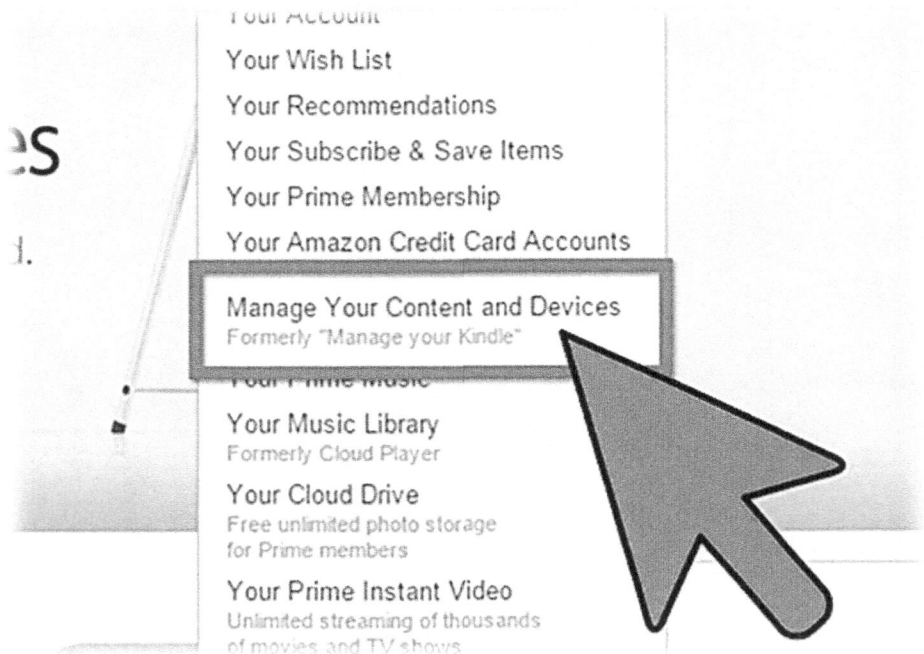

Go to "Content and Devices Management." You must sign in to your online content library on the Amazon website to delete an item permanently from your Kindle content library.

- To begin, open a web browser. Visit the https://www.amazon.com/mycd page for your content and gadget online.
- To view this page, you need to log in to your account.

2 Ensure that the "Your Content" tab is viewed. You should See under the "Your Content" tab when you sign into your account. To view an item in your library, click on the 'Your Content' tab. If you look for a different tab instead.

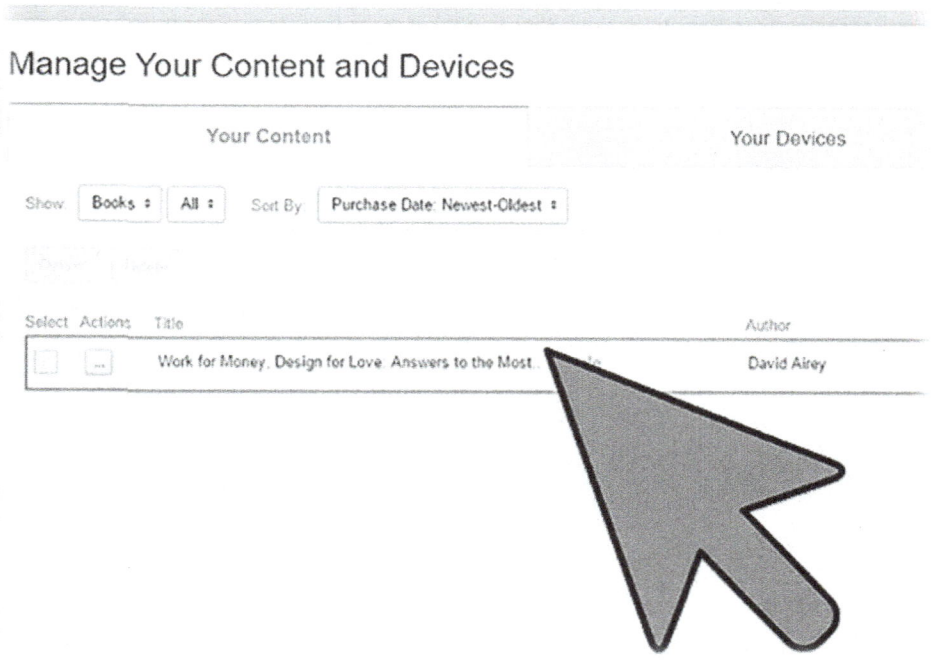

3 You can select the removed book(s). Under a column labeled "Select," you should see blank boxes at the far left

of your screen. The box you can tick for a book is in each row. Check the box next to the books to be deleted.

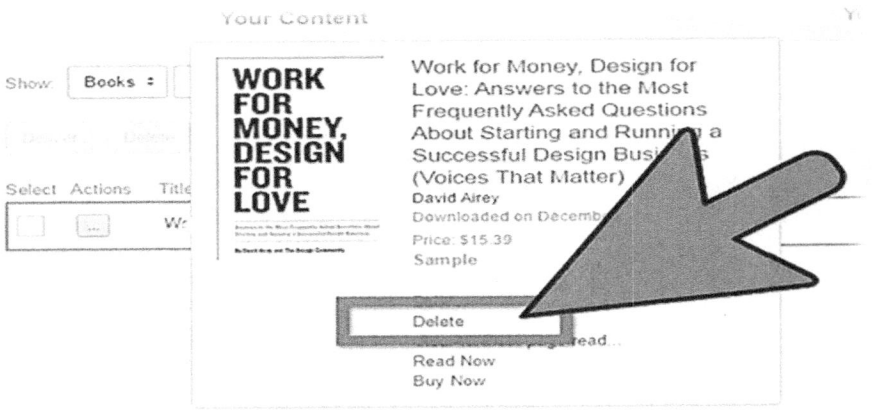

4 Touch on the delete button. On the page top left side, you should see a "Deliver" orange button and a 2nd "Delete" orange one. To delete the chosen items, tap on the "Delete" button.

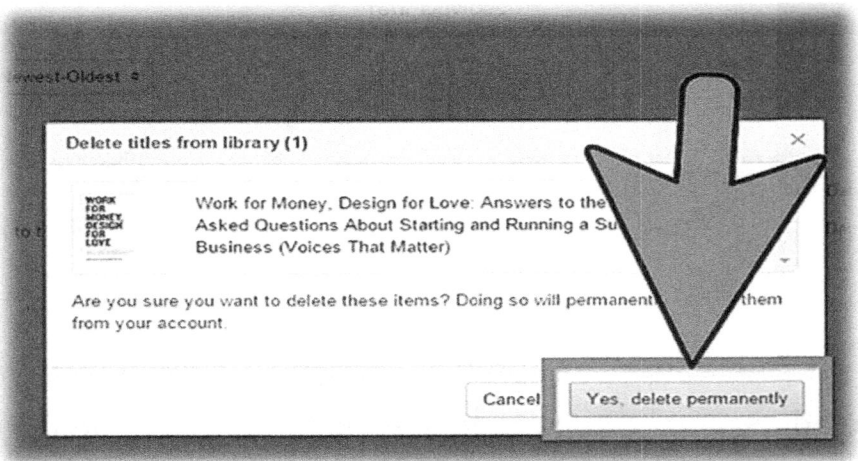

5 Confirm that the chosen items you want to delete. By choosing "Yes, permanently remove," you will need to indicate that you would like to delete the book. You must click this button to remove the items from your library. Another box will show what you have just erased. When you see this box, just click "OK" and it will disappear.

6 Sync your devices. You only have to sync your gadget to remove books that you lately removed from the Kindle library. You need the following requirements to synchronize your device:

- Take or click on the Kindle icon on your device screen to open your Kindle application.
- Tap the top-right of the screen three points. Tap.
- The sync & check for items option is giving in the first item. The book(s) will be removed if you tap on this item.

Method 2 Wipe books off from Kindle

1 Go to home screen. You can gently drag your finger up and down on the screen to access your whole library.

2 Find the title you prefer to remove. Find the title that you want to remove by scrolling up and down. Tap the glass loupe icon at the upper right of the screen if you don't find the title. You can type in the title or keyword and search your device for the title.

3 Hold and delete the title. Once the book that you want to delete is located, press the icon with your finger and hold it until the screen menu displays. Hold on and you will see a menu on the screen for a few seconds. The menu will provide you with multiple options, including one that states "Device removal."

- By touching on it, select this item from the list. Click on "Device removal" to remove your Kindle device's book.
- Be aware that the item will remain in your Cloud after you have removed an item from your Kindle device. You may therefore download it later if you like.

Method 3-Books on Kindle Archive

1 Tap the home symbol to the Home Screen. By holding down the power button, you can turn on your gadget. Press and hold the power button for a few seconds when viewing

Kindle in a portrait direction. Shortly after you release this button, your Kindle will start.

2 To navigate your collection, use the 5-way controller. Once you find that title, ensure it is selected by being highlighted.

- 3 On your 5-way controller, press the right direction. The action list is displayed by pressing this button. The option "Remove from Device" can be found at the bottom of the action list. Come down to this option using your controller. Once you have been certain that your book is being archived, tap the "Remove from Device" button at the center. Archiving simply removes the item from your device, however, it keeps a purchase and downloads record.
- Restore an archived item by moving to your Kindle "Archived items" section on the screen. Then press the center button to download the content again, scroll until you locate the title you want.

Method 4 Kindle Deregistering

1 How about you deregistered your device. If your device was stolen or lost, the easiest method to make sure that all

your items are no longer on that device is to unregister the device using your Amazon account. If you want to resell your device, this is a fantastic choice. Keep in mind that all items from Kindle will be withdrawn when you unregister this device and that, until you reregister this item, you cannot access it on this device.

2 Go to "Content and Devices Management." You may see the option "Manage your contents and devices" by hovering over your account button. If you want to access this page, you must sign in to your account.

In addition, visit https://www.amazon.com/mycd to view your content and devices page online

3 Choose the "your device" tab. Once you have logged into your account, select the "Your Devices" page once you click on it. You should see a list of gadgets registered in your accounts when this page is opened.

4 Select the gadget you want. Select the device by tapping on or clicking on it once you want to deregister. The device has an orange contour and a pink background if selected. There is nothing around the other gadgets.

5 Click on the button "Deregister." On the left of your screen, you find the Deregister button directly below your list of devices. Click or press this button once after you are sure that you have selected the appropriate device.

When you tap or click "Deregister," the connection between your Kindle and your Amazon account is disconnected. You will remove any books you purchased from your Kindle. Upon registration of your Kindle on another Amazon account, you can only then be able to download or buy content.

How to print

Method 1 Kindle eReader Printing

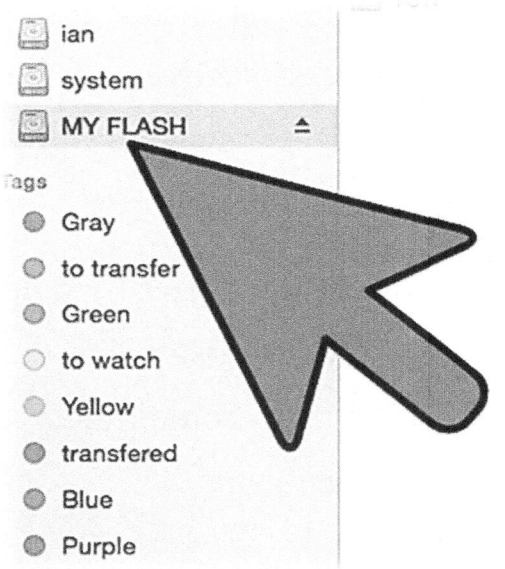

1 Plug into a computer. In contrast to the tablet-based Kindle Fire HD, a normal Kindle system does not do beyond showing ebooks. You can still print documents, but you first need to hook them up to a computer as usual. Connect the Kindle through a USB cord to your computer. Your computer should register a connection between the Kindle in a few seconds.

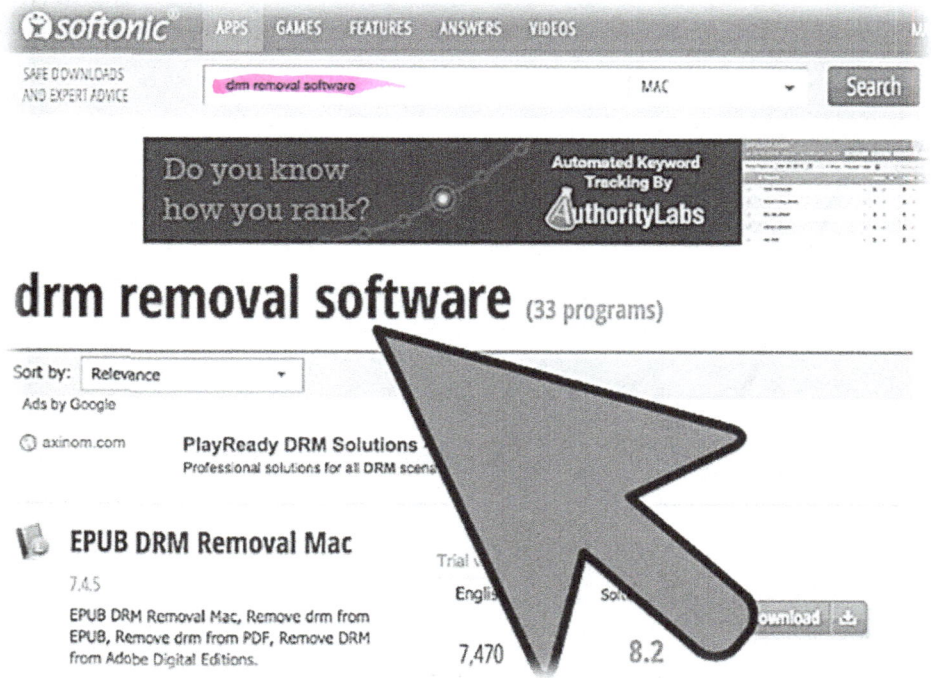

2 Install in your machine DRM removal software.

Kindle-bought books have copyright protection to avoid excessive dissemination, limiting file copying and physical printing. This is annoying but can be circumvented using software from third parties. Fortunately, it is easy to get DRM removal software. Download and install a Kindles-based DRM removal application on your computer. Ensure that you download from a well-respected source. Where the download has an excess of marketing or special offers, it may be dangerous and worth looking for an alternative.

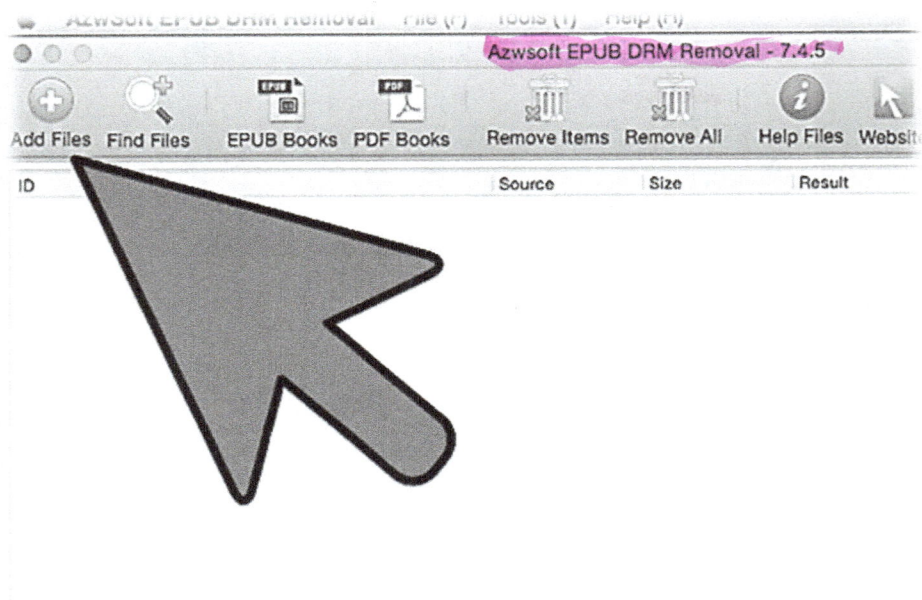

3 Decrypt the Kindle files and copy them. DRM removal applications make a replica of the selected ebook file with no copyright protection, leaving the originals unchanged. Otherwise, the file should be the same as the original. Upon installing your removal software, access the program and pick the file(s) you want to print. The application copies the files and removes them from the DRM.

4 Convert format. Cracked files can be converted (Kindle uses a single .azw format) to .epub or .pdf with a PC tool such as Kindle. Although you cannot print a .azw file on your PC via a Kindle, converting the file from an application that has a printer function, such as Adobe Reader, will permit you to use the file. The Mac OS also offers similar programs. Check OS compatibility before downloading an application.

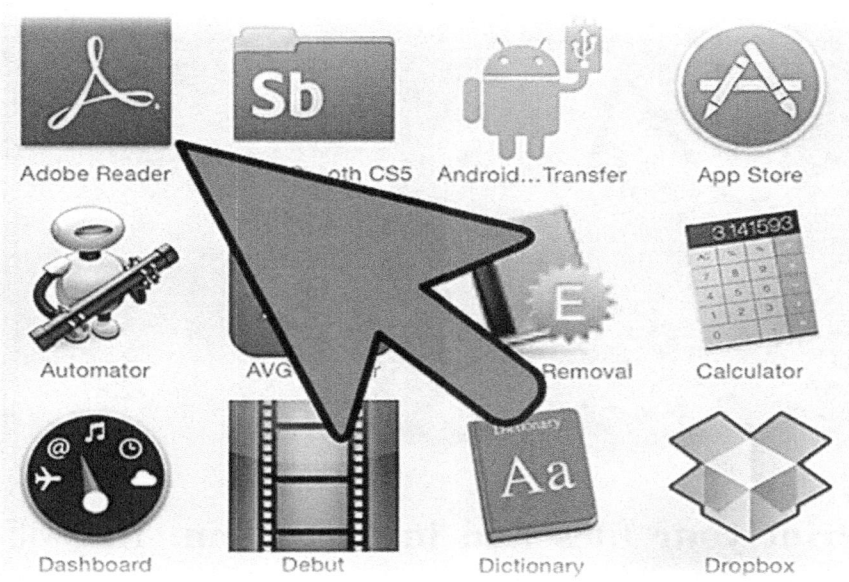

5 Choose from a print-friendly application the files you want. It should be quick and easy to convert files via Kindle for PC because e-reader files are usually pretty small with design. A third-party reader such as Adobe Reader or Calibre should be accessed from there. Locate the file that you wish to print out once a universal reader application is running. From there a print button should be visible.

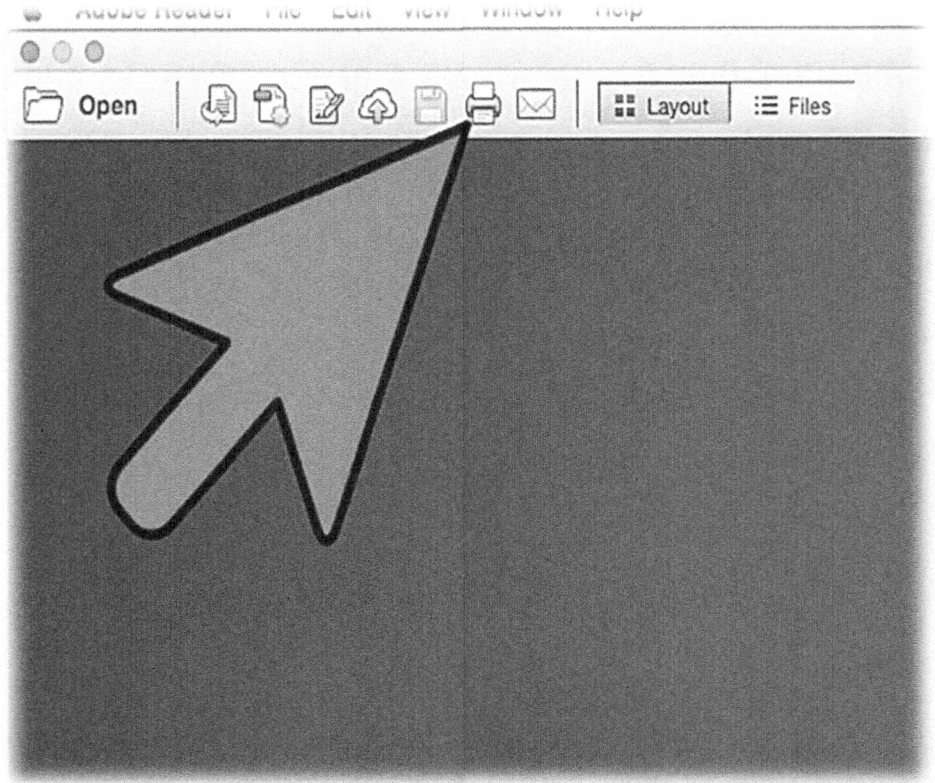

6 Print your files and inspect them. You will be encouraged to type some print information when you click on the printer button, including the number of copies you want to make and whether you want the pages to be created on either one side or two. Complete the correct information and complete the printing procedure. The print should go through as scheduled, provided that the connectivity of the printer is stable and appropriately supplied with ink. Once the pages are all printed, verify them successfully for printing. Compare the number of pages and make sure that all pages are inked appropriately. If you plan to print out a larger file, you may need more cartridges. If you print a complete book, it is recommended that your pages be double-sided, because this facilitates the binding of pages.

PDF in Kindle

Method 1-Transfer PDF through email

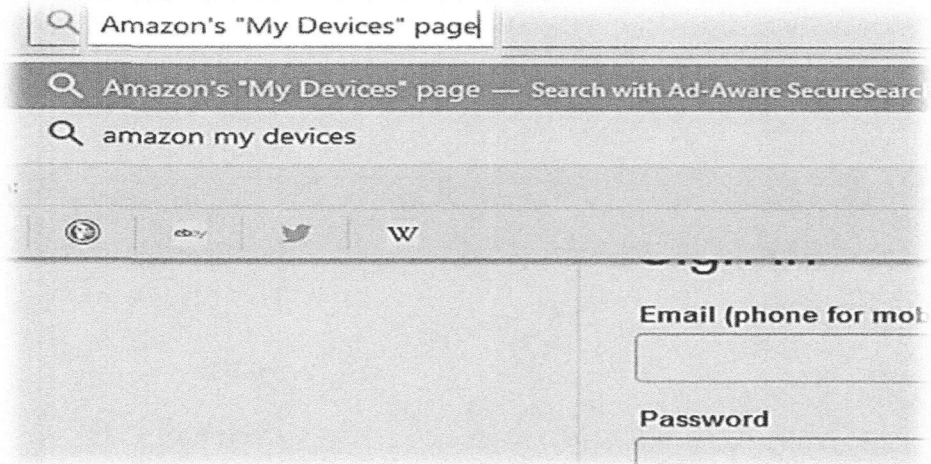

Search your email address for "Send-to-Kindle." You will send the PDF to your Kindle or Kindle application with the following e-mail address:

- Open and sign in, if required, on the "My Devices" page of Amazon.
- Click the Personal Document Settings which can be found as you scroll down.
- Check the email address in the heading "e-mail address" and scroll down.
- If necessary, add a New Email Address by tapping on Add new Approved email, type in an email address when requested, and click Include Address.

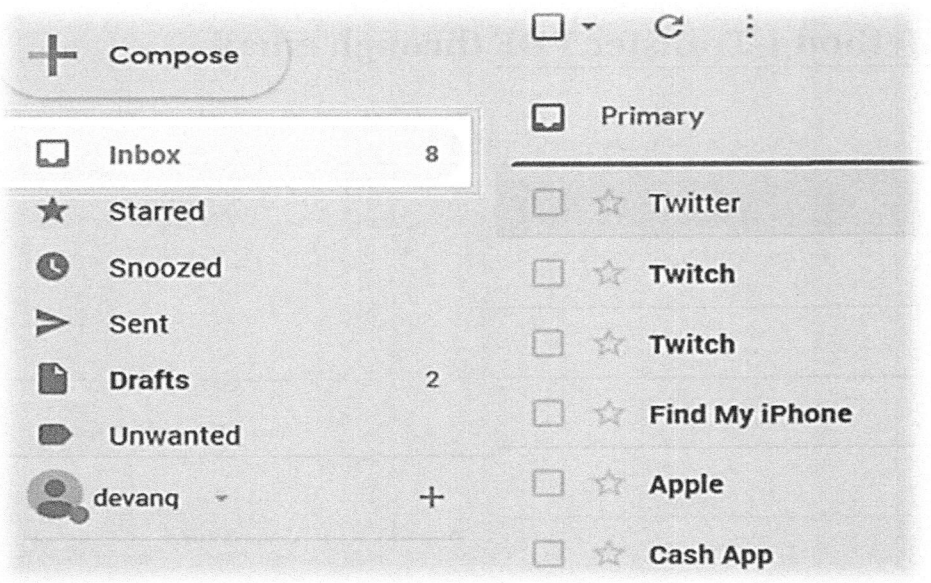

2 Open the inbox of an email. Go to any email service you have an account with. You will need to enter your email address and password to log in if you are not automatically logged in to email services.

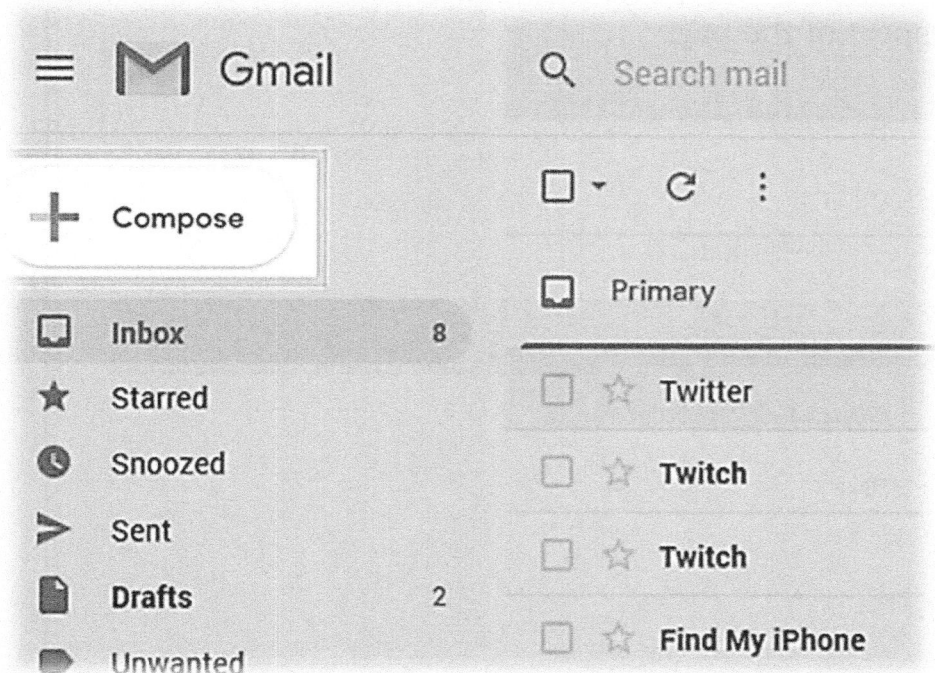

3 Make a new email, create a new one. Open the "New Email" window according to your favorite email service by doing the following:

Gmail — Click COMPOSE on the left-hand side of this page (or, if you use the new Gmail Inbox, + Compose).

Outlook — In the upper left corner of this page, click + New Message.

Yahoo – In the upper left of the page, tap on compose.

iCloud Mail — Tap on the blue "Compose" icon in the top aspect of the page.

4 Input your "Send-to-Kindle" address. Enter the E-mail address you discovered on your Amazon account's Kindle page in the 'To' text field. In this area, enter the 'E-mail address.

5 Click the icon marked "Attachment." It is normally at the bottom of the email page or the top of it. A File Explorer or Finder (Mac) window will be displayed by clicking on this icon.

6 Choose the PDF you want. Please click on the PDF file to select the PDF on your computer.

7 Click Open. The window is in the lower right corner. Your email will include the PDF file.

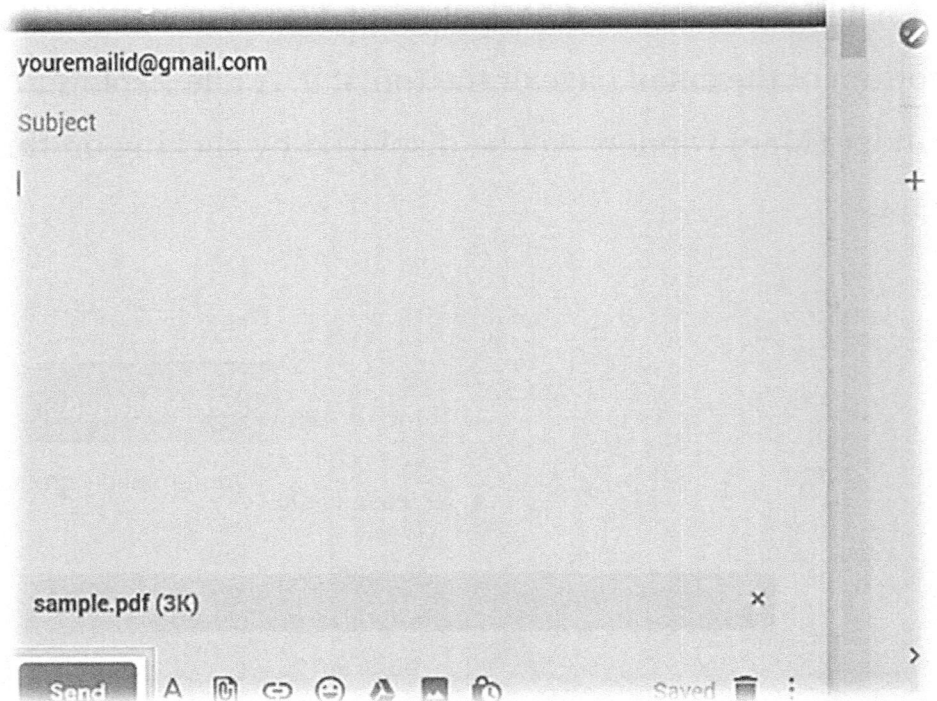

8 Send your email. To do it, click the Send symbol (or plane-like paper icon). PDF will be sent with this to your Kindle or Kindle app. The PDF may take few minutes to display.

You may be requested to send an email in the "Subject" and the body text boxes, depending on your email service. To confirm that, click Yes or Send.

9 Open the Kindle PDF. Enter the "Library" part of the Kindle and see the PDF, then make sure your Kindle is unlocked and connected to Wi-Fi (or to the cellphone). You can tap it to choose it once the PDF comes here.

If you are operating the Kindle application, you can open it and sign it in if necessary. To access your Kindle files list, hit the LIBRARY tab. Upon PDF arrival, you can tap on the PDF icon.

2 Method-Download PDF using USB

1 Don't utilize this procedure for the Kindle app. Use the e-mail technique instead if you want to put a PDF on the Kindle app on your tablet.

2 If operating on a Mac, download and install Android File Transfer. Since Mac computers are unable to access Android file systems on their own, Android file transfer is necessary to install to bridge the gap:

- Go in your web browser of Mac to https://www.android.com/filetransfer/.
- Click on the DOWNLOAD NOW button.
- Click the DMG file you've downloaded.
- Click and drag the icon to transfer the Android file to the folder 'Applications' icon.

3 Copy your PDF. Go to your Kindle PDF position and click the PDF and hit Ctrl+C (Windows) or Command+C (Mac).

4 Connect to your PC your Kindle. Connect the USB end of the cable charger to one of the USB ports of your computer, then plug the 2nd end of the cable into the charging port of your Kindle.

5 Open the folder of Kindle. This step varies according to the operating system of your computer:

Windows- Launch File Explorer (or press the Win&E), then left-hand click the Kindle name. To view the Kindle here, you may first need to scroll down the sidebar.

Mac —Open Android File Transfer instantly. If not, open it with the Macspotlight.png and dual-click Android File Transfer via android file transfer to Spotlight Image.

6 Open internal storage of the Kindle. If you cannot open the Kindle immediately in a list of folders, double-click the folder "Internal" or " internal Storage " to open the Kindle folder.

- If you are using a Mac Skip this step.

7 Search for and open the folder "Docs." This is the directory where you can store files from your Kindle, for instance, PDFs and Word documents. Open it by double-clicking. This directory may be called "Documents" if you upload the PDF onto the classic Kindle.

8 Paste PDF. Once you have opened the "Docs" folder, click on Ctrl+V (Windows) to add the copied PDF to the folder. This puts your PDF in the Kindle.

9 Eject your Kindle and remove it from your PC. You can remove it from its cable after carefully ejecting your Kindle.

10 Open the PDF. Open the "Library" part of the Kindle to see your PDF. You can select it to open when the PDF appears here.

How to connect a TV

Method 1- Fire TV Connection

Buy Fire TV from Amazon. Get from your local electronics store or online an Amazon Fire TV stick or an Amazon Fire TV box. If you purchase HD6 or 7 Fire, HDX or HDX 8.9, HD8 or HD10, or 2nd generation HD devices, you may connect to Kindle.

- An Amazon Fire TV Stick links to the HDMI connector on your TV using a dual-core processor and one GB of storage. It enables you to watch more than 250,000 TV and movie episodes and offers music and games.
- Amazon Fire TV Box is much larger and has certain software and hardware changes than the Amazon Fire Stick. It is USB-supported with gaming systems and USB gaming and remote 3rd-party controllers. You can wirelessly or if wired also connect to the internet. There are also 2 GB storage and Bluetooth-compatible peripherals such as headphones, keyboards, mouse, and remote devices.

Connect to the Internet. Internet connection. The connection to Kindle via Fire TV is subject to internet access as well as to the Amazon username. The Fire TV and Fire tablet must be linked to and registered for the même Amazon login on the same Wireless network.

Use a default HDMI cable. Buy online or at your local electronics store an HDMI cable. Connect it to your Fire TV device from your HDMI connection. Use the Fire TV device and type 'Settings,' then move to display & Sounds' and choose "On" Second Screen Notifications' and select.

Fire tablet usage. Find a video or picture slideshow on your television. Use the display icon, which appears like an arrow in a box. Check your Fire model as some will give you the choice to link to your TV via "Settings," next "Display & Sounds," for "Display Mirroring.

Setup Bluetooth connectivity

How can I know whether my Kindle has Bluetooth?

Tap the Menu bar close to the top of the screen. Choose Settings, which gives you a list of available functions on your gadget. It means your Kindle does not support Bluetooth communication if the Bluetooth symbol is not there.

How can I link Kindle Paperwhite to Bluetooth headphones?

In this section, I will use a Kindle Paperwhite to create and pair Bluetooth headphones.

All these gadgets perform the same essentially, i.e. scan and pair with your device. When you realize how to set up one, the others are quite the same.

The reason for connectivity problems in most cases is two:

- Maybe we did not activate Bluetooth on one or both devices.
- Both devices have stopped pairing thus you have to rescan.

Let's begin with our Kindle PaperWhite's Bluetooth enabling.

1. We have to go to the top of the screen main menu, and press Settings.

2. Extends the menu, now the Bluetooth symbol should be viewed.

3. The Bluetooth is not active if the icon looks darker than the rest. To enable Bluetooth just tap this symbol.

4. Once activated, the Wi-Fi and battery icon should display a smaller icon at the top of the menu bar.

5. Now Bluetooth is configured and enabled to pair with another gadget.

Kindle Bluetooth and headphones Pairing

We are now trying to connect your Kindle Paperwhite with Bluetooth headphones.

- Tap All Settings in the Settings section.
- Choose the wireless internet & Bluetooth option.
- You must see the Bluetooth switch set to "On" to establish that your Bluetooth is enabled. If not, just hold on to the enable switch.
- Choose Bluetooth devices. Tap this option.
- The Bluetooth Devices window will now be displayed, with a Rescan Button in the underneath right corner of the window.
- On your Bluetooth headphones, press and hold the Power button.
- Now the headphones are trying to combine with the Kindle.

- The device ID should be presented when the Kindle has found the headphones.
- To couple, the devices together, tap the Connect button.
- You now have the headphones associated with your device Kindle.
- You can do a variety of things from here, for example, hear your Audible books or read an ebook using Whispersync. You can read several things.

I suggest you try Whispersync if you have not tried yet, since it is a free excellent service for users in Kindle, just make sure to do it on your online account with Managed Devices.

Please note that only ebooks with voice-over are available. On Amazon, you may search to discover if this feature is in your ebook.

Bluetooth Troubleshoot

What should I do, Kindle Paperwhite is not pairing?

Things aren't always as smooth as the preceding scenario.

Here are some things to check for your device to connect.

1. Be sure headphones is powered

In general, the majority of Bluetooth headphones have a power indicator that indicates they are on. If you haven't been using your headphones for some time, it could be they have run out of power. In such a scenario, before you try to pair, you will need to charge them. I'd say that 30 minutes is enough to charge.

2. Activate Pairing

A scan button may be used on some headphones or speakers. Follow your manufacturer's instructions to begin transmitting a signal to the Kindle device. You normally have to wait 2-3 seconds for a scan to be done.

3. Do a Rescan

Both devices typically transmit 1-2 minutes of signal and deactivate pairing afterward. Therefore, you need to make sure that you set your Kindle and power your headphones in the first minute. That gives you more chances to connect gadgets successfully. If this fails, tap on the Bluetooth Devices pane to retry the rescan button. I would recommend at this point that the headphones be repowered to guarantee that both broadcasts.

etooth scanning on a Kindle device:

- Tap Rescan at the bottom left corner of the Bluetooth Devices window.
- You should now notice the Bluetooth scanning text at the upper left corner together with a circular rotating progress icon.
- Press the power button to turn it off and then press and hold it until it is turned up again, turn the power on your Bluetooth headphones. The headphones have power, according to light.
- At some time your Device ID or Name should normally appear with 10-20 seconds.
- Tap the device name and you will see a tick icon on the right hand side of the Device ID, provided the two device pair successfully.
- Both smartphones are successfully paired now. Time to rejoice! Time to celebrate!

Wi-Fi Connection

To wirelessly connect your Kindle Paperwhite:

1.Select Menu from the Home screen.

2.Select Wi-Fi Networks and Settings.

3. A list of discovered wireless internet networks will be displayed here. You may need to wait a moment when you identify networks in your Kindle Paperwhite.

4. Tap a connecting network. A network password is necessary if you see a lock icon.

Kindle will recognize your Wi-Fi network and router which supports WPS. To connect to your router, press the WPS association button from the required Wi-Fi password screen. Input the Wi-Fi network password if your network doesn't operate WPS. Contact the person who set up the Wi-Fi network if you do not know this password.

Tip: Enter numbers or symbols by taping the 123 key. To come back to the usual keyboard, tap the ABC key. To enter the high-case characters, tap the Shift key (up arrow). No non-English letters are allowed in your password (accents, umlauts, etc.).

Once linked to a Wi-Fi network successfully, when your Kindle Paperwhite detects a signal from the Wi-Fi network it will automatically reassemble. If several previously used networks are available, your Kindle Paperwhite connects automatically to the network used most recently.

Borrowing library's books

If you want to read Kindle Books from your library Kindle devices or Kindle Read apps, you can borrow.

Note: U.S. libraries only

How to borrow and supply books

- Open a digital collection for your library (you can find it using www.overdrive.com).
- Find a book for borrowing from Kindle. By selecting the link Kindle Books towards the top, you may view the Kindle Books of your library (or under the Menu icon on mobile devices).

Note: before you borrow a Kindle Book, you may wish to examine if there are any device restrictions (you can encounter this for picture books, read-along, and graphic novels).

- Choose Borrow. Borrow. Sign up in your library if requested.
- Choose a title loan period (if available). Then again choose Borrow.
- Now select Read with Kindle after borrowing the title.

- To complete the ebook acquisition, you'll be transferred to the website of Amazon.

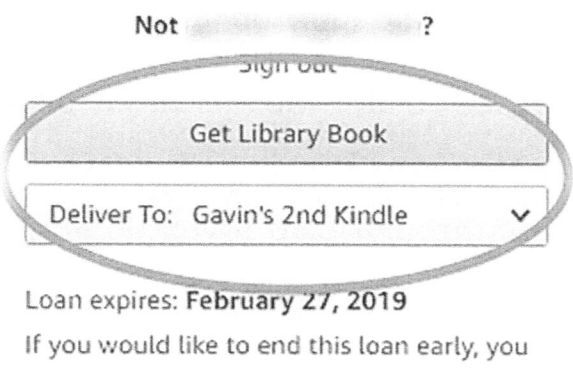

Note: This step is required in order for your rented book to appear on your Amazon account in the "Your Contents and Devices" list. You won't be able to download this book on any device if it doesn't appear in this list.

1. Check the "Deliver to:" device and pick Get Library Book, if you have signed in to your Amazon account.
2. Select Get Library Book and sign up if you have not registered into the Amazon account.

A Wi-Fi is needed to download Kindle Books from the Amazon library for your Kindle e-reader. You will need to transfer the title through USB if you do not have a Wi-Fi connection. You can read it like any other book when you have a book on your Kindle device or application.

Send books from Mac

Try out the Send to Kindle App if you're sending your Kindle more and more files from your PC. Both Mac and Windows can access and use the app for free. With the Kindle eReader or the Kindle reading app on your other devices, you can simply share documents and book files immediately. Here, we will show you how to use Send to Kindle to transfer your products to the Kindle app from your computer or to view them.

Send from Mac to Kindle

Installation of send to Kindle

You can directly get the send Kindle app via Amazon. Download it onto Mac or PC and follow the instructions on the machine to install it. Subsequently, register the app in your Kindle's Amazon account.

The sending program will be shown on Mac in your Dock by default. This makes it incredibly easy to use since you can drop files on the icon right away. But that's not the only way to utilize the program, of course. If you would like to remove this from your dock, click it right, move to Options and choose Remove from the dock.

Change the options

Sending to Kindle doesn't have much to worry about, but you may wish to enable one in particular from the beginning. This setting converts PDF documents to Kindle format automatically.

1) Launch Send to Kindle.

2) Tap on the options button.

3) The General tab is selected.

4) Check the Convert PDF to Kindle format box.

5) Hit ok.

You're never going to have to worry about the wrong formatting of your PDF in your Kindle by activating this configuration. You can check any other items if you want and close the Options window when you are done.

Explore Send to Kindle'

The Send to Kindle program on your Mac has a few useful ways to use it. You can pull objects to it, transfer items via Finder, or utilize the print menu through an app. We're going over it all here so that you may utilize the app however you prefer.

Use the App to Send: Drag and Drop can be used to send documents or books with Send to Kindle. Drag your file immediately to it if you keep the icon on your Dock. If not, open the application and drag the file to its window.

Transfer from finder: Right-tap on the item in your folder and touch Sending to Kindle.

Sending through the print menu: It is easy to utilize the Print menu to move documents such as PDFs. Pick

Send to Kindle and click the Print button in a Printer drop-down box.

Note the statement from Amazon concerning the manner of the print menu:

You can send a document version larger than the original via the print menu.

Send the Item

Whichever method you pick, the identical pop-up window will be sent to you.

1) You may wish to modify the title and/or author, depending on the item.

2) Select the device(s) and app(s) you want to send.

3) Choose the archive box for your Kindle library to download when you are ready.

4) Send click.

As the item is uploaded and a confirmation completed, you will see the progress pop-up.

Move iPad Books to Kindle
Step1: Wipe off DRM from iPad books

- First of all, connect your iPad through USB to a PC. Together you will see iTunes on your PC. Yes, the purchase of your iPad books in this library is saved. Here you may find the default directory path easily: \My Documents\then Music\ iTunes\iTunes media/ next Books Music.
- Download Requiem and use it to erase DRM out of iBooks.
- You will obtain all of your iPad non-DRM books after completion. They can be converted into any size.

Step2: Convert Kindle Books

- ebook converter should be Downloaded and installed to help convert books, such as epub, pdf, and mobile, from one format to another.

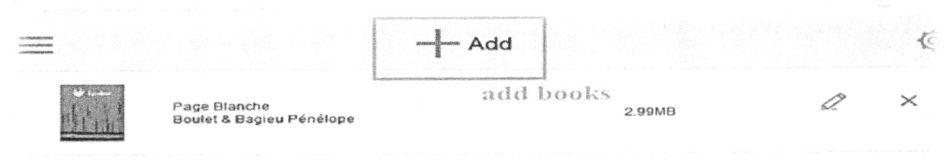

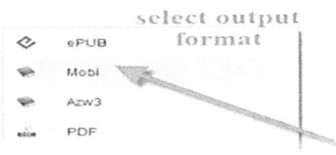

- Click "Add" to select the DRM libraries you have received in step 1. Select the correct Kindle "mobi" format for output when you have added books. The conversion will start soon, just click on the "Convert to" button.

Step 3: Move books to Kindle

- You get books in the pop-up window once you've converted books to Kindle format.
- Connect your Kindle device via USB connection (or your friends, daughters, husband, etc.). You'll see "Kindle" on your PC. You may simply copy your books from the output folder to the Kindle "docs" folder.

How to move Kindle books through iPad

- Kindle App on your iPad must be installed. Then purchase your preferred books.
- You only need to wi-fi your Kindle, sign up for your own Amazon account on your Kindle device, go to your library and all books on iPad may now be synchronized with your Kindle.
- This is only an addition to you. Naturally, for this section, the above steps are still available. As iBooks are transferred to Kindle, just be sure your books can be converted.

Synchronizing Kindle to iPad

1 Start the Kindle application on your iPad and input inappropriate places the Amazon.com username and password for your account. To register an iPad app in the Amazon.com account, click the "Sign In" button.

2 Start your computer's Web browser, navigate to Amazon.com's homepage and press the "Sign In" button.

3 Enter the credentials of the same account you used when you registered your iPad with the Kindle App and select "Sign In."

4 Tap on "Your Account then click on 'Manage Your Kindle' in the 'Support Kindle' part.

5 On the left-hand side of the website, click on the link 'Manage your devices.'

6 In the Whispersync device synchronization portion of the page, tap on "Turn On".

Create Kindle Child profile

In case your Kindle is in Amazon kids, move to the menu and choose Children's Exit Amazon and include another child profile by entering your parental control pin.

- Tap the Home screen menu icon.
- Choose Amazon kids.
- Choose Add New or Add Child Profile.
- Enter your pin code for parent controls, if necessary, the name and birthday of the kid.
- Select any content that you wish to include in your child's library from your personal library and then select Next.
- Select Done after you review the profile of the child and read the setting.

Edit Child Profile

Would you like to make changes to your child's content? Update the Amazon Kids profile on your Kindle.

- Choose the menu icon from your home screen.
- Choose Amazon kids.
- Next to the kid profile, choose the drop-down menu. You can adjust several aspects of the profile of your child, including your age, education level, and book sharing.

Bookmark and Highlight Content

It is easy to sign and highlight contents via Amazon's Kindle 2. Amazon wishes that you can do all things that you normally want to do, like "dog ear" or highlighting a page, to make reading books and any other content on a slide as much as is feasible like reading a regular book. You can quickly find your favorite sections with only a few clicks when you use these tools.

- Open a book and turn on your Kindle 2. Automatically, the book opens to the last page you read.

- Put the cursor where you can emphasize the text. The cursor can be controlled with the 5-way controller from the Kindle.

- Press the 5-way controller and move the cursor to the end of your desired text. The starting point of the highlighted text is locked by pressing the 5-way controller.

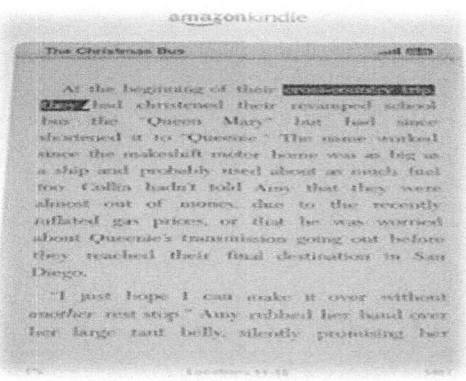

- At the end of the passage, hold and release the 5-way controller. A little darker background will lie in the highlighted text than the other text around it.
- To select several pages, hit the Next or Previous Page buttons to proceed to the endpoint of the passage.
- Go back to the book page and click on the menu. Although the Kindle saves the page which you read automatically, you may want to make bookmarks at different text area in the book to return later.
- Use the 5-way controller to create bookmark.
- In the My Notes & Marks list available in the main menu, the bookmarked page will display. By moving the preferred page and hitting Alt-B you also can create a bookmark.

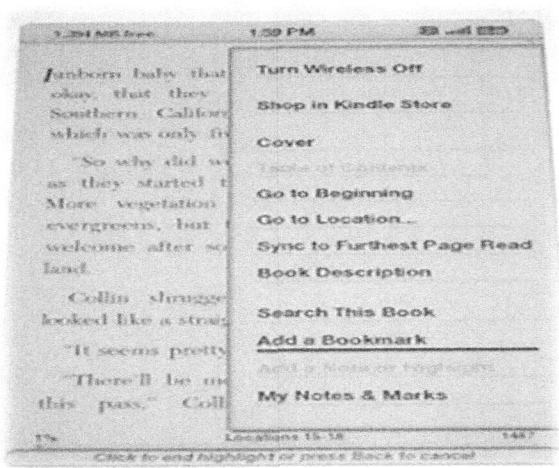

- Click on the Home button and then move forward a few pages and select my notes and tags. A new bookmark will appear and you will see the selected text in a list.
- Press the Delete key and highlight the bookmark. The same procedure is used to remove notes or marks from this list.

- When you're finished, close the menu and return to where you stopped reading.

Word Wise

Word Wise is a great tool for individuals reading difficult literature, language learners, or those who wish to improve their vocabulary by providing brief and easy definitions for mundane and complicated words. It's is only available on Kindle and Android Kindle app as the desktop version does not support it.

[This is an instance of Word Wise on a Kindle device]. Word Wise's beautiful in that you don't have to tap the word to acquire its meaning. In addition to the dictionary, Wikipedia, and translation tabs, the definitions are shown on top of every word and a term are listed. If the term has more than one meaning, you have other meanings and you can alter the meaning of a given word with Use this meaning. It's not 100% accurate and sometimes it has wrong definitions and it's advisable to double-check if you are not sure of the interpretation.

It could be annoying to a few people because, depending on the dial settings, it emphasizes simple words too. When you click on the WordWise button below right when you read, you can decide how many hints you want to see, a popup from Fewer Hints to More Hints should come with a 5 level slider, along with the option of hiding WordWise hints. Setting the slider to fewer hints shows only the most challenging definitions, I think, makes the reader less aggravating.

To enable Word Wise on Kindle, go to the Aa menu in a book and select More where extra read options and change Word Wise settings can be customized: language and multi-choice tips.

Kindle PaperWhite reset

1. Make sure that you have a full battery before proceeding

2. Tap the Menu button with your powered-on the device, which displays in the right top corner of the screen as three horizontally stacked lines.

3. Tap "settings."

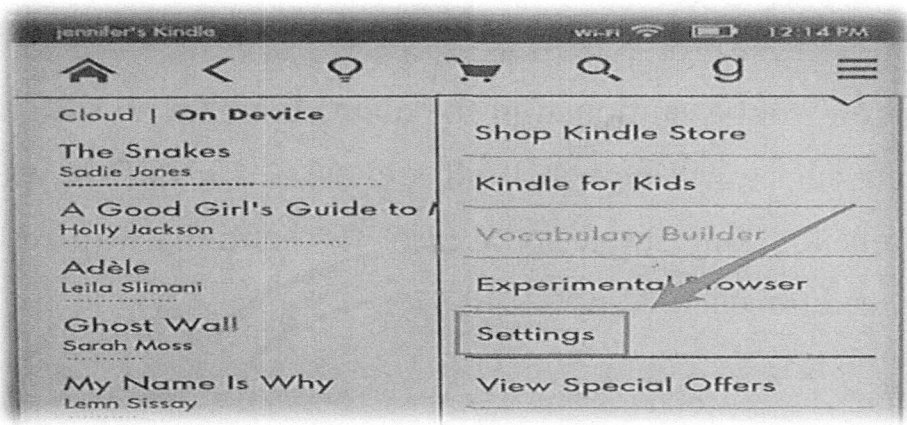

To begin resetting the device, tap "Settings."

4. Tap Menu again, then click on "Reset Device" on the Settings page. Tap "Device Reset."

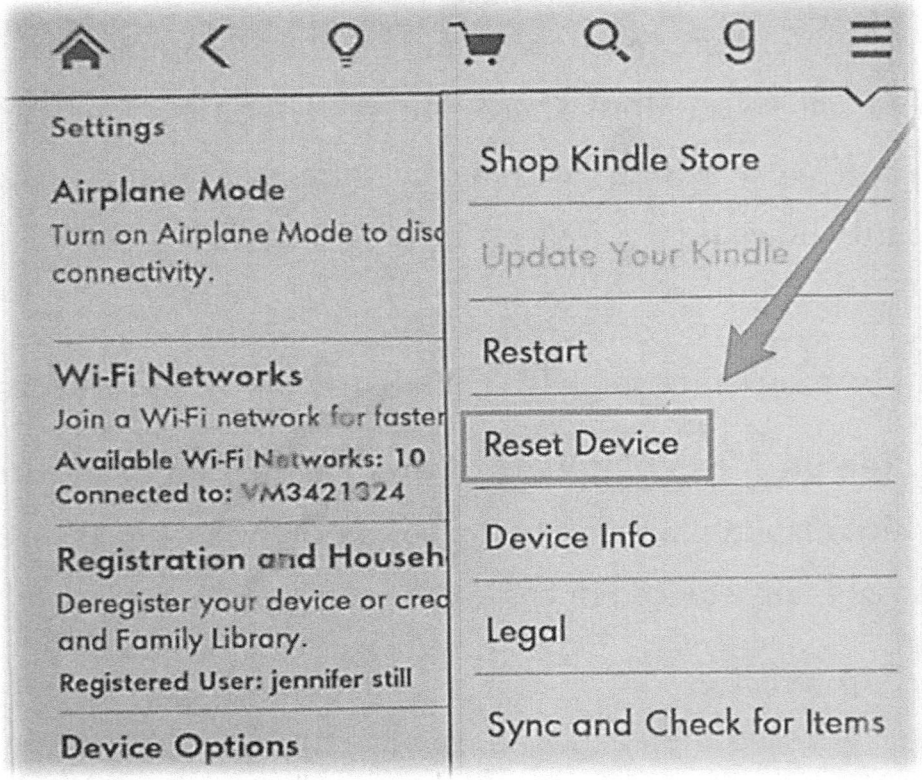

5. You will be cautioned in the dialog box that all data on your device will be wiped off and asked to confirm your intent for your device to be reset. To continue with reset procedure, click "Yes."

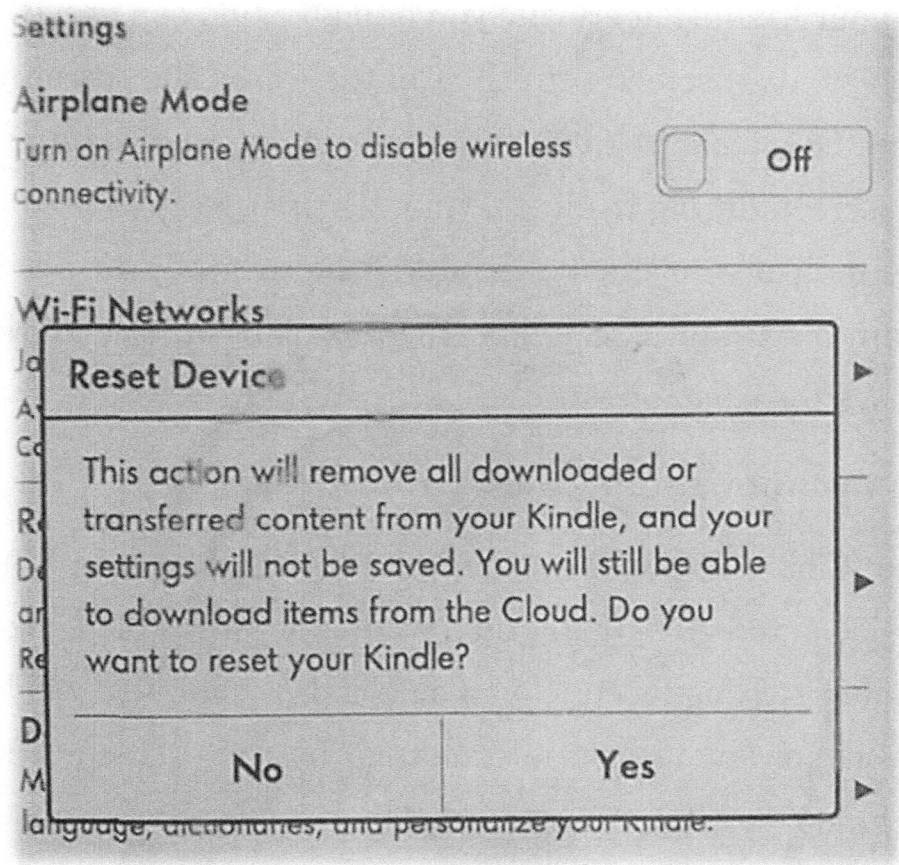

Troubleshooting

Here are some of the more common issues mentioned in community forums by Kindle Paperwhite owners. There are steps to quickly resolve many of these difficulties.

Ghost Images

Ghosting is a tiny display of text and graphics which persist from a previous page even after going to the next page. If on your Kindle Paperwhite you find ghosting of a previous display, do a screen refresh. Tap the top of the screen to view the toolbar, then tap anywhere on the page, to refresh the screen during reading. When the screen refreshes and the toolbar vanish, the display flashes briefly in black. From the Home screen, opening a book or other material makes the page refresh.

You cannot automatically connect to Wi-Fi

The Kindle Paperwhite detects Wi-Fi systems in your device automatically. If you find one network, the gadget immediately connects. If you need a password, you will be asked to enter this information by the screen. The technique is often fast and simple.

However, you may sometimes need to manually connect to the Wi-Fi network. Follow the following steps:

- Tap Menu
- Click Settings.
- Tap on that network if the network you wish to connect to is on the list.
- You're done!

If there is no indication of the network you want to connect to:

1. Tap Other. In addition to the on-screen keyboard, a box term Enter Wi-Fi Network is displayed.
2. Enter the network name and password using the onscreen keyboard.
3. Tap Advanced.
4. Work through series of displays and enter network information, including connection type, IP address, and preferred security. Navigate with up and down arrows through the screens. Contact the person who set up the network to support the supply of this information as necessary.
- Tap the Connect button to connect to the network if all the relevant information is inputted.

You may have to reset your connection if your Kindle Paperwhite is linked to your home network but cannot connect with Amazon. Tap Menu Settings for the Wi-Fi network and tap the network to the left. Tap Forget when it displays in the Forget Network dialog box. The network is re-selected and the password is entered (if one is required).

If you can't connect to home network, unplug your Wi-Fi router, wait for a minimum of 60 seconds, then plug it in and wait for your network to restart.

Synchronization not working

Amazon's Whispersync function allows you to switch smoothly from reading on your smartphone or your computer. In addition, Whispersync for Voice can be synchronized with an audible version of your Audible app between your Kindle PaperWhite and a book you can listen to on a favorite audio device.

> Sync to Furthest Page Read
>
> You are currently at location 4567. The furthest read location is 4575 from "iPhone 2" at 3:30 PM on August 23, 2013. Go to that location?
>
> Cancel   OK

Usually, you can move to the most distant position while opening the ebook on the other device. Check the following if this is not the case:

Connection to the Amazon server: The devices must be connected to the Amazon servers for Whispersync to function. Ensure you have a wireless or 3G link while synchronizing your Kindle Paperwhite or other devices.

Sync settings: If Amazon's servers are connected to your devices and sync still does not operate, check your sync settings. Log in and go to your Kindle Manage page in Amazon. On the left-hand side of the page, click the Manage your devices option. Scroll down to the bottom of the page to check that the sync option is enabled.

The synchronization setting affects all your account-related devices and content; you cannot activate or disable Device Sync selectively for a given device or e-book. If you have more than one e-book Kindle (for instance, your spouse and your children's Kindles) and everyone reads the same e-book, the Kindle syncs for everyone to the last page read. In this situation, the synchronization may be disabled.

In the Manage Your Kindle book, you can reset the last page that you read. Click the Actions box next to the corresponding title. Select Clear Furthest Page Read from the drop-down menu.

If the Home screen is not organized

You can show news, titles, authors, or collects on your home screen. Most times items are not shown in the correct pattern.

Make a fast resync to prevent this issue:

- Touch the Home screen Menu icon.
- Check for Items after ta Sync. The fifth option on the drop-down is Sync and Check for items (fourth option for the second-generation Kindle Paperwhite). Your home screen displays items properly.

Make sure the clock is in the right position on your Kindle Paperwhite. To automatically change the clock you can set the Kindle Paperwhite 3G.

Your password does not match the device

To protect your Kindle Paperwhite access, you can use a password. You have a few troubleshooting alternatives if your password for your device doesn't work:

- Make sure that you accurately input your password.

- Try a few password changes. Perhaps when you first set it up, you mistyped it.
- You should input the password on the right device if you have more than one Kindle in your household.

Hopefully, one such problem-solving step will help since it is extreme to reset your password. This solution eliminates all content and removes it from Amazon from your Kindle Paperwhite. It may be possible to reinstall all your material, but it takes time. Type 11122777 in the password field and then press OK in order to reset your password. Your bowl is smoothly wiped. Now you have to re-register Amazon's gadget and download content from your Amazon archive as requested.

Freezing Issues

Like any technology, on your Kindle Paperwhite, you may sometimes suffer freezing or delayed reaction. The solution is usually straightforward. If your Kindle stops responding, try these methods.

An e-book will not open or stop answering

If your Kindle Paperwhite freezes or begins to behave oddly when you reading one or more e-books, try restarting the menu and do a hard restart if necessary. The file could be corrupted if these solutions do not work. If so, remove the item to see if the problem is solved. If you've purchased the book from Amazon, remember that it will be saved in the Cloud and downloaded again. Make sure you've got a backup before uninstalling the book from another source.

Remove the product from your Kindle Paperwhite using the following steps:

- Tap and hold the item from the home screen.
- A several options pop-up menu is displayed.
- Tap Deviate or Delete This Sample option Tap Remove (for samples).
- Your Kindle Paper White will erase your eBook or sample.
- Press and hold the power button for about 40 seconds to restart your Kindle Paperwhite (7-15 seconds for a second-generation Kindle Paperwhite).
- Try to see whether symptoms have cleared up by reading other contents. If you do, you can try downloading Amazon's e-book again by selecting it on your Home screen from the cloud or sideloading it from your computer to your gadget.

The system is freezing or very slow.

Use menu restart or a hard restart to resolve the problem if your Kindle Paper White stops behaving at its usual quick pace.

Start by restarting the Kindle Paperwhite menu:

- Tap Menu.
- Move to settings
- Tap Menu, then click restart

(From the drop-down option, restart is the 3rd item) The start-up screen and progress bar are shown in your Kindle Paperwhite. The smartphone restarts and displays the Home screen after a minute or so.

Try a hard restart if the menu restart does not solve the problem:

- Press the power button and keep it down for about 40 seconds (7-15 seconds for a second-generation Kindle Paperwhite). The display becomes blank.
- Push the power button again – just press the simple button as if you're sleeping out your Kindle Paperwhite. A shadow child reads underneath a tree

on the startup screen. The gadget starts the restart procedure in a few seconds and displays a progress meter. You can view the Home screen when this restart is complete.

The unusual behavior of Kindle Paperwhite might be because of low battery. If you still have troubles, plugin and recharge your device for at least an hour, then try rebooting by menu and then do a hard restart if needed.

Made in the USA
Monee, IL
25 February 2023

28694084R00057